I Want to Meet Your Light

Ben Gallup

Copyright © 2019 by Benjamin Gallup

ISBN 978-1-7339661-1-5

Cover design by Benjamin Gallup

Cover photograph by Adriana Cordova

Tox Typewriter font by junkohanhero

Contents

I Want to Meet Your Light	1
Wake Up!	3
Church	5
Little Beauties	7
That Kind of Friend	9
No Rest	12
Honor	13
She Was Glorious	15
Birds	19
I've Been Hurt	20
I Am a Ghost	25
My Head	27
So Far from Your Feelings	29
The Young Construction Worker	32
Don't Be Shy	34
If You Really Want to Know	35
The Digger	38
White Genocide	41

I Could Tell He Never Saw Me	45
Reminisce of the Present	46
Kindness	48
Safe	49
You Just Can't	50
No Compensation	54
Silence Is a Gift	56
Stood Up	57
The Shit Talker	59
Whatever You Do	61
Who Are These Artists?	65
Young Love Forever	66
The Mess	67
Firefly	68
A Blessing for You	71
Why?	74

I Want to Meet Your Light

I Want to Meet Your Light

I want to meet your light
right at the front
of your eyes,
bright,
unclouded,
shining from deep in your center
where the hearth crackles.

I want the light to meet me
right out front
and invite me inside,
unafraid.

You'll know it's safe
because my light will meet you there
at the doorsteps of our worlds.
And you will see clearly
into me too.
And you'll see that I don't want
to take anything
or change anything
or condemn anything.

You'll see that
I just want to like you.

You'll know it's safe
because my eyes
will be warm and opened to you,
trusting that you too will move
with care and mercy
as you come through my wilderness
to join me
at my fire.

Wake Up!

If we were truly awake
to what matters in life,

we would
play and laugh, enjoying just each other
with uninhibited delight,
because we love each other so much;

we would
savor the unfolding instants,
soberly staring into each other's eyes,
cursing and praising time,
because we love each other so much;

we would
meditate together
on the truth that we will have to die,
grieving and sobbing and wailing
and pressing our bodies together,
hating to let go,
because we love each other so much;

we would
break every politeness and taboo against
expressing love,
break our fear of loving too much,
break our fear of being loved too much,

break our hearts open,
purposely and urgently and desperately,
knowing everything depends on this,
because we love each other so much.

We would,
if we were truly awake
to what matters in life.

Church

Earth,
most Holy Church of churches,

people pissing in the pews,
windows either broken out or boarded up,
cigarette butts stomped into the floor,
and that pile of shit and garbage
that people started in the corner
is starting to spill all over the place.

Gah!!!
Don't they know this is a FUCKING CHURCH?!

No, they don't.

Our ancestors all knew
but now most of us have been trained
not to notice.

And soon enough we will all die
of starvation, dehydration, violence, poison, or sickness,
corpses strewn and piled
quiet and still
in every room.

The church will go on standing,
but what good is a church
if no one worships there anymore

Little Beauties

Find little beauties.
Take a closer look.
As your focus narrows
the object expands
beyond measure.

What was once a discrete object,
limits defined,
is now a world without end,
just as Earth is a neat, little sphere
from far away
but on the ground, it is an intricate plane
stretching off into infinity
all around you.

Wander across the vast, vast
leaf.

Hike the peaks and valleys
of the texture
of paper.

Everything is strange and wonderful!
...except for those old ideas
that make up the walls
of the little room you live in.

The deadness you see in the world
is only the deadness of your withered ideas
reflected back at you,
which you mistake for reality.

Clean your eyes
and let them receive
the vitality and intelligence
of the endless and alien
construction of the cosmos
on display
in all the little beauties.

That Kind of Friend

I have some great friends,
people I actually relate to.
They're always available.
They never get possessive or jealous.

They are extraordinary people,
one-in-a-million kind of people.

My friend,
Carl Sandburg,
has been telling me all about Chicago
and making me fall in love with it.

My buddy,
John Reed,
has been telling me all about what he saw
during his days in Russia
when the workers and peasants
took power from the rich
and started forming their own government.

My new acquaintance,
Rilke,
well...
you would just have to meet him yourself.

But as much as I love these friends,
these people I connect with,
they can't help me
when I really need a hug,
when my skin needs to feel
someone else's skin,
feeling mine,
feeling theirs.

They're not that kind of friend.

That kind of friend
is so hard to find.
You can't just pull them off a shelf
when you want them
and put them back
when you're done.
They have feelings
and needs and desires.
They deserve accountability.
You have to earn their trust
over time
before they really let you see
what's behind the cover.

Why do I have so few of these friends?
Do I lack patience?
Am I too quickly bored or disgusted
by the introductions?

Am I too suspicious
they will try to stitch me into their binding,
like others before have?

At the beginning of my life,
just after I learned to walk,
I learned how to read.

And yet after all these years
I still feel hopelessly bewildered
and ineffective
at finding and enjoying
human companionship.

No Rest

We can't be present for the bliss
of blessed self-forgetfulness;

we can't savor even a peep,
awake in precious nightly sleep;

and release from Earthly grieving
arrives just as mind is leaving.

Honor[*]

I can't always feel cool,
but I can always be authentic.

I can't always feel attractive,
but I can always take care of myself.

I can't always get a hot date,
but I can always abide by consent.

I can't always find the comfort of human connection,
but I never have to settle for people who bring me down.

I haven't always made a decent living,
but I've never taken advantage of someone to get paid.

I can't always stop people from controlling me,
but I can endure as I plan my escape.

I can't always get what I want,
but I can always abstain from selfishness.

I can't always avoid frustration,
but I can always be kind to the innocent.

---

[*] Originally published by The Good Men Project

I can't always be happy,
but I can accept necessary suffering.

I can't always avoid mistakes,
but I can always be truthful with loved ones.

In every situation
we can choose
shame or honor.

Honor.
Honor.
Honor.

She Was Glorious

She came into the coffee shop around 8:30pm.
I think she was about 70 years old.
She had put in effort to look nice,
with a beret cocked off to the side.

She was looking for dinner but
this coffee shop was not really a place to do that
but she didn't know.
She struggled to understand her choices
and asked questions about what sauces might be
available.

I understood her disorientation and embarrassment
and grasping for anything to help her figure out
which way was up and which down,
and where the ground was and
how to appear competent.

I remember moving to the big city,
a working class, rust belt kid
feeling small and panicked,
intimidated and uninitiated, ashamed
in the bourgeois coffee shops
trying to figure out how to order "coffee."

This barista was cold and impatient and
entirely lacking compassion,

unable to sense
the woman's feelings and needs,
unable to put her at ease and simply
feed her.
She didn't understand.

I felt like I knew this woman.
I know the kind of stale
museum-of-her-whole-lifetime
apartment that she lives in,
which nobody visits.
I know the suffocating stillness and
changelessness.
I know the fucking miracle
of courage and defiance it took,
determining to go out into the world,
to put herself together
and look nice and
put on her beret
at a snappy and stylish angle
and walk out there
into a public space in a city and a world
that she once knew so well,
which she had spent a lifetime nourishing,
which used to have smiling, familiar faces and
conversations, and
warmth and it was home
but now it has moved on and she is lost,
just trying to figure out how things work
as she walks into a cafe
seeking plain food that she understands

and this barista
is incapable of helping her feel welcome,
feel the ground under her feet,
feel a simple, human connection in her face,
and just get her some food
that she would like to eat.

Ma'am, I don't know your life.
Your life is not my life.
But I know something of your sadness and
I LOVE you and
I am here in your world with you!

We know how it feels
to quietly understand
and accept
the failure of hopes.
We know how it feels
to quietly understand
and accept
the calloused hearts.
And we know that the barista is lonely and anxious too.
And we have compassion for us all.
And the tender, sweetsad love
that took anger's place years ago
when it burned itself out.

Why,
knowing we all struggle with loneliness
and self-love,
do we not embrace each other?

Why
do we distract ourselves from tragedy
instead of helping,
or even add more misery,
to an already too-mean world?

Why
are basic love and connection and community,
these most human of all things,
so scarce?

Birds

I have seen a bird
cowering, shivering, shy.

I have seen another bird
extending its wings,
pushing on air until it rises,
then finally soaring,
riding on nature's invisible currents.

I've Been Hurt

1.
I've been hurt.
Real bad.

No, I'm not trying to compare.

Everyone has a right to honor their own wounds.

And everyone has a responsibility
to go to their pain
and heal it because
hurt is contagious.

It helps to talk about it a bit.

I don't remember
what happened.

I remember bad things
but I can't find the memories that explain

it.

I'm sorry.
I always feel like I need to apologize.
I'm a walking apology.

Sorry.

I feel like I need to apologize for being born
but no matter how much I apologize for it
I never feel forgiven
enough
to live
my life.

2.
I've been hurt
real bad,
somewhere deep where my mind isn't allowed to go.

But I feel it
when I speak
or dare to try something
that would require me to believe
I can belong.

I feel it
when it swells up
and spreads through my body and I
deflate
and clench and contract and shrink away
like I'm trying to protect myself from another blow

or just disappear.

I used to use anger to get big and strong
and push everything away
and get enough space to
be.
But I burned through my lifetime supply of rage
in just a few years
and now I live with the regret of
scorching people around me.

I used to use alcohol and drugs
for the soothing
and the cheap, fast illusion of power,
but each night's step forward
cost me two steps back.

I finally found myself
but I was miles behind.

3.
So
I stopped taking the edge off.
Now I want to leave it on.
I need it to cut this mystery open.

I've spent years trying to give myself permission to
cry.
I can do it a little now.
It feels useless trying to squeeze a river
through a little crack.

But I remind myself that
one little crack is all it takes
to bring the dam crashing down
some magnificent day.

4.
Patience.
Persistence.

Patience.
Persistence.

Patience and
persistence
of water.

Water's ease and assurance, effortless
in awesome weight and power,
in inevitability.

5.
And I will burst through that wall,
taking the spaces that are mine to fill,
with innocent confidence,
trusting nature
will continuously correct my course
as I flow freely into my life,

laughing at my silly self
for ever having been a river
who wanted permission
to join in our ocean.

I Am a Ghost

I am a ghost.

Sometimes I drift through the city
among the living.

I observe them
going through their motions.
They can't see me.
They hardly see each other.

It is lonely to haunt,
to see and not be seen.

But, ah! the thrill
of encountering another ghost!
The relief and longing fulfilled
as our eyes meet,
crossing the distance in less than a blink!

We move towards each other
through the crowded graveyard.

At last to be seen!
And by such a spirit.

One who saw the dream behind the illusion,
One who wasn't strong enough to submit

but had all the courage to rebel,
One who smashed their tight shell,
One who cut off their Earthly anchor
for freedom to pass through walls
and see the other sides,
adventuring through worlds and times!

How sweet it is to have found each other!
But
we ghosts can no longer become anchored,
even when we want to.

Knowingly, we drift our separate ways.

But we are eternal
and we look forward
to meeting again
and again.

My Head

If you walk up to talk to me
you won't notice the size of my head
because it's just about the size
of a human head.

But inside
I can never seem to reach the walls of my skull.
In fact, it's so vast and open in here,
I think it goes on forever.

There are dark, bottomless holes
Bizarre mazes
Huge cities
Impossible architecture
Countless people
Strange people
Mysterious forests and oceans
And suns and moons
And solar systems
And new universes and dimensions are always
opening up.

And in here I have total freedom.
Flying is a very minor miracle in here.

And though you're standing there
looking at my head in the present moment,

the time inside my head
goes way back before the beginning
and far, far beyond the end of so-called "time".

I don't often look out
the windows of my eyes because
what I see in here is usually much more interesting.
(But I know, I know...I should get out more.)

I just want you to know all this because
if you come knocking
it might take me a little while to answer.
I may have to make quite a journey to get back
to my front door
and I probably have to throw on my bathrobe real
quick.

And I might seem a little disoriented
when I answer.
I prefer to have a little time
looking out the windows
before I try to interact with anyone.
I need a little time to see and remember
what it's like out there
and how I'm expected to act
so that I don't come off as rude
or crazy.

So Far from Your Feelings

Hello Dearest,

How can you stand to live
so far
from your feelings?

All alone out there in the world.

You never visit.
You never call.
You never write.
When we call
you never answer.

I know you're busy
but some things you have to make time for.

We miss you.
At this rate we're going to become strangers!
Would you even recognize Joy if you two were in the same room?
I hate to tell you
because I don't want you to worry
but
you really ought to know.
Joy is very sick,
withering away almost to nothing.

But remember the twins, Loneliness and Resentment?
They've grown up so big since the last time you saw them!
You'd have to see them again to believe it!

I understand that
you had to move away for a while,
get some distance,
find yourself,
but it's time to come home
and give your feelings another chance.
You moved away so young;
you only knew us through
a child's eyes.
But you've matured now and
you'll see us in a whole new way.

Won't you come home,
even just for a holiday,
and get reacquainted?

Don't you want to hear everyone's stories
and learn about where you came from?
It's never too late to come back
but each day that passes without us
is time you'll never get back.

And each day
you'll have the vague torment
of missing us.

Love,
Your Feelings

P.S. We're just going to keep bothering you until you come home.

The Young Construction Worker

The young construction worker
asked the older construction worker,
"¿Al lado?"

Ah, I was jealous.
The young man,
just becoming a man,
young.
His honorable, hard work.
He and the older man had a familiarity with each other.
There was a hierarchy
but the hierarchy itself
hinted at a deep and loving bond,
larger than two men.

The young man was deferential and humble
to the elder,
which did not indicate weakness
but rather
made the youth more venerable and dignified.
It indicated his path,
rites along a definite road to maturity,
learning how to be part of something
bigger than himself,
something alive
but older than any living individual,

something that he is gradually taking
responsibility for,
ensuring its patterns
of love and survival
will continue to be woven
long after he himself has returned
into the ground.

The young man
looked so bright and hopeful,
earning a living,
maybe in love,
maybe excited to start a family,

a most precious piece contributed
from each of two ancient families,
who are now moving together,
gathering around
as a new living shape is born
into the greater mosaic,
lawfully shifting the sacred geometry
of family and eternity.

I was so happy for him but,
ah, I was so painfully jealous
as I walked past them
on my way home
alone.

Don't Be Shy

Just those three old chords,
no less, no more,

those simple but perfect words,
familiar, yet never heard,

and that honest voice like a friend,
have saved my life again.

If You Really Want to Know

How are you today?
Suffering deeply.

How are you today?
I'm experimenting with what it means to live without fear.

How are you today?
Last night I rode out a terrifying storm, withstanding winds and waves I thought would throw me into the dark ocean to drown alone. I survived. Today I can see that the storm was only in my imagination.

How are you today?
I've been plummeting through the abyss for so long that now it just feels like I'm floating here.

How are you today?
I've just returned from the void and I'm soaking in so many strange and wonderful sensations!

How are you today?
I'm remembering that painful feelings are always temporary.

How are you today?
I really miss my family.

How are you today?
Meow meow meow meow,
meow meow meow.

How are you today?
UUUUUngh! bee bee boo bao!

How are you today?
Full of explosive, destructive fantasies...
I'm not angry...
I just need to see *something* change.

How are you today?
I'm lonely.

How are you today?
When I'm feeling unlovable I hold onto a memory of
my grandma smiling at me.

How are you today?
Desperately looking for a sign of life
in this wasteland of hungry ghosts.

How are you today?
Did you know
there's a scientific consensus that
you will see,
with your own eyes,

the masses of humanity all dying
terrible deaths,
almost all at once,
as you die too?

How are you today?
I really need a hug.

How are you today?
"How"?
"Am"?!
"I"?!?!?!

How are you today?
Oh, I'm good.
How are you?

Digger*

I'm always digging
I don't know why I can't stop.

Maybe I always want to know what's underneath.
Or maybe I'm never satisfied with what I see.
There's got to be more.

Sometimes I see a glint down there
or imagine what's below those
unremarkable surfaces
and then I just can't help it:
I dig.
I'm a digger.

You can always uncover a new space.
Sometimes it's bright under there.
Maybe part of me knows that the only way out is through.
Maybe there's another sky down there.
So I dig.

Often I want to go wandering out wide
and sometimes I do.
But mostly I dig.
Intently.

---

*Originally published by Rebelle Society

I'm getting somewhere.
Maybe a wiser part of me knows
the greater adventure is to go in, inner,
in-est.

"Sorry,
I'd really love to see you tonight
but, um, actually
I have this really important digging thing I have
to work on..."

Maybe I can't help digging through the past,
piled up and decomposed.
I extract nutrients,
organic matter reduced to elements
that can become new life,
old materials to combine in new ways.
I find artifacts
that can help me see my way backward
and forward
at the same time.

Maybe some part of me remembers that,
while I've tried so hard to build myself a
certain way,
the real me
was already built
Perfectly
but got buried long ago,
and its excavation is now an emergency.

Or maybe I'm really just looking for a simple home,
a place to plant myself.
Maybe I'm a seed.

So often I ache to rise
to new heights.
Instead I just keep digging down deeper.
But maybe a wiser part of me knows
like a tree does
that you can only reach higher if you
stretch deeper.

Maybe I'm digging a well.
Maybe I'll strike the aquifer
beneath all forms,
feeding each variation into being.

And one day,
after a lifetime of digging,
if nothing else
I'll have a grave
and I'll crumble into it,
graceful,
grateful.

There's dignity and purpose
in digging it yourself,
starkly aware
that is what you are doing.

White Genocide

Who are you fools
whining about "White genocide"?
Don't you know that Whiteness
was
the destruction of our European cultures?
Whiteness isn't our tradition;
Whiteness erased our tradition.

Don't you know that to become "White"
your German/Nordic/Celtic/Welsh/Polish/
Slovenian/Italian
ancestors
were forbidden to speak their own language
and made to speak English?
Don't you know they had to
stop talking "so loud"
and have "some class"
and "act right"? (i.e. White)

Their traditions were erased
and replaced
with White.

This is why
White people are a people who don't know
who the fuck we are.

This is why
we make up myths about homeland,
Columbus, pilgrims, Jefferson, Manifest Destiny.

When the world hears you
talk of "traditions" that are a few
hundred
years old,
they laugh
because they see that you have
no idea
what it means to have traditions.

The first attack on our traditions came long ago.

Don't you know that your ancestors
became Christian at the point
of a sword?

Don't you remember?
Your traditional religion
was terrorized out of your village
when the Christian priests came and
burned your spiritual leaders at the stake
for all to see?
Don't you know our ancestors were
forcibly assimilated into a culture
of empire, war, and hierarchy?
Maybe it is our culture now but
don't mistake it
for tradition.

And your homeland?
You and I lost all connection to homeland
when the rich
forced our ancestors from the
green commons,
and into gray, urban tenements
to become fodder for factories.

And after what our ancestors suffered,
when people today are forced from their land
and into hazardous and inhumane factories,
you don't stand in solidarity with them and their
resistance.
You want some of that land!
You want to own the factory!
(Or at least become a manager!)

But you'll probably just remain a struggling
worker,
though you'll have the fool's consolation
of being White.

You are a shame
and a betrayer of our ancestors and old ways.
Their blood, and the blood of the world, is on your
hands now.

If you had any true generational memory
of your traditions
and their erasure
you would live a life of war

against Whiteness.

And no, don't move to Norway
and try worshipping Odin.

We can't go back,
only forward.
And we need to start now,
not quibbling over who we were
but deciding
what kind of people we want to become.

And we need to do it
in humble and sincere collaboration
with everyone else,
so we can all decide
what kind of world we want to become.

I Could Tell He Never Saw Me

I could tell he never saw me
because his sight couldn't reach me,
because it stopped before it left his eyes.

I could tell he never saw me
because his sight couldn't reach me,
because his spirit couldn't shine
past the clouds
in his pupils.

I could tell he never saw me
because his sight couldn't reach me,
because the pure and tender lens he was born with
had been scarred over
by the violence of his experiences.

I could tell he never saw me
because his sight couldn't reach me,
because his inner light couldn't escape
the gravity of his own pain
and hunger and rage and despair.

I wanted to help
but there was nothing I could do;
he couldn't even see me,
because he couldn't see anything
outside of himself.

Reminisce of the Present

Here I am
back in this life
on Earth
as a human.

Here I am
back in this body
with this name.

Here I am
back when I looked like this.

Here I am
back in that old home.

Here I am
back before they died.

Here I am
back before she and I recognized
we were meant to live our lives together.

Here I am
back when I had so much turmoil and confusion about
what I should do.

Here I am
back before I knew
how it would all turn out.

Kindness

Kindness is not submissive.
It is comfortable in its strength.

Kindness doesn't shrink.
It is its own size.

Kindness doesn't condescend.
It con-ascends.

Kindness doesn't contrive a smile or sympathetic look.
It expresses itself through a face that can yield to the movement of inner sincerity.

Kindness doesn't enable excuses.
It supports success.

Kindness isn't always nice.
It is sometimes even fierce.

Kindness isn't a gift you make to give.
It is a by-product of grace and love
found through your own struggles.

Kindness isn't an attitude toward others.
It is realizing that there is no such thing as others.

Safe

You thought you locked your feelings
in a little box.

But now you realize
you've played a little trick
on yourself.

You've locked
yourself
in little a box,
and you're afraid to come out
where the wild feelings roam.

You Just Can't

You told her you would
kill someone
for her
if she asked you to.

You went up to her and said,
"Gimme a hug,"
but when she said,
"No, estoy bueno,"
you grabbed her anyway.

You told her to do things
and threatened her not to disobey
and when she disobeyed
you grabbed her by the hair and
yanked her head back.

You were jealous that she had
another friend
so you stared into her eyes
and said,
"You're lucky I don't have my knife
right now."

And when she told the teacher
you sent someone to tell her
she owed you an apology

or else.

I know you want a friend
desperately,
that you want to grab her and hold her
and never let her go.

But you're hurting her
and you're not going to get
what you want
that way
anyway.

You can't scare or hurt someone
into loving you.

You can't make someone love you.

You tell the kids you're going to Coachella
and that your dad is giving you
thousands of dollars
to buy clothes.

But
you can't lie or fake someone
into loving you.

You can't make someone love you.

I wish you could see that
you don't have to do anything.

I wish you could see that
we already love you.

But as long as you
threaten, hurt, and lie to people
they will have to love you
mostly from a distance.

I'm sure you understand
that people have to protect themselves.

But they will give you many chances.
They will be patient.

It will take time,
courage,
experience,
test after test after test
before you are ready
to trust the world.

I know you will.

But it will take time,
courage,
experience,
test after test after test,
before she will be ready
to trust
you
again.

Most importantly,
my young comrade,
I just want you to know that
we love you
and we won't stop.

You can't make someone
stop
loving you.

No Compensation

An excess of one kind of strength
indicates
weakness somewhere else.

Find where you have become too strong,
rigid, brittle,
and you will find your weakness
in its shadow.

Compensation does not correct the imbalance.

It reinforces the imbalance.

It is a temporary solution,
an emergency measure to save you from disaster.
But left uncorrected
it becomes its own disaster.

You are soft in ways you should be stronger.
You are too strong in ways you should be softer.

Let your brick walls breathe and stretch.
Let them become flesh again.

Seize your weakness.
Plunge it right into your frenzy of fears.
Let it stay there and struggle

and tear and resist and persevere
day after day.
Let it become strong like a tree,
bending with every wind
and always returning to impeccable posture.

Life needs structure to flow.
Life needs structure to flow.

Silence Is a Gift

He'll say it's childish that
you won't talk to him,
because he knows this started with his latest
infantile tantrum.

He'll try to explain things,
but you know he only has self-serving delusions and
excuses.

He'll say he wants to resolve things,
but he doesn't care about resolving anything;
he just wants to feel better.

You'll be so tempted to talk to him,
trying work things out,
but you keep quiet because you have wisely given up.

You'll be tempted to let it all out
just as you're leaving for the last time
but your silence is your last gift to him
--a lifelong reminder that
if he ever wants anyone to stay close
he has to stop acting like a monster.

Stood Up

Getting stood up for a date is like

no one showing up for your birthday

or

finding out you've taken the bait in a prank and everyone is laughing

or

realizing you've been lied to by someone you naively trusted

or

realizing there's a joke about you that everyone knows but they've been trying to keep secret from you

or

feeling like you've done something wrong, though you meant to do something good, and now you're ashamed you didn't know

and

remembering that many people have no sense of honor because they have never known the feeling of being honored

so

you renew your vow to treat all people with respect and kindness.

The Shit Talker

The shit talker
talks shit
because he's insecure.

The shit talker
acts cool
because he feels like a loser.

The shit talker accuses you
of the things he hates
about himself.

The shit talker
has been hurt
and you don't know his whole story
but you understand enough
to sympathize.

You've felt insecure.
You've felt like a loser.
And you've been a shit talker too.

You see,
the shit talker talks shit
because he believes he's shit.

Somewhere deep
he still believes the shit talkers
who told him that.

He was a perfectly sweet and innocent kid.
But thanks to those shit talkers
he now sees a threat where there isn't one,
sees a fight where there isn't one,
and so he fights
but doesn't realize he started it.

He's become the shit talker.

And when he realizes this
it's going to be hard for him to accept.

If he still can't forgive himself
for being shit,
which isn't true,
it will be much harder to forgive himself
for being a shit talker,
which is true.

So you be patient
and you love him like yourself,
which you are finally learning to do.

Whatever You Do

In Seattle
people obey the "don't walk" light
at the street corner,
even when no cars are coming.

It's strange to see them standing there,
obeying without thinking,
but how many signs do we all obey
absent mindedly,
without pause?

Signs,
symbols,
words,
flags,
facial expressions,
emotions,
thoughts.

Signs only have power over you
if you don't reflect on them.
Reflect on them and
take your power back.

Maybe that guy is wearing that cross
because
he's an ally to the poor and oppressed,

or
maybe he's just exploiting that symbol
so he can exploit you.

Don't trust a sign.
Meet the substance.

Maybe that flag stands for freedom
or
maybe genocide, slavery, and imperialism
or
maybe all of these and more.

Maybe it's not so simple.

A sign is a very simple thing
but significance is
precisely
the opposite of simple.

Maybe that look means
she doesn't like you
but
maybe she likes you a lot
and it makes her nervous
or
maybe you're irrelevant
and she's had a hard day
or
a lifetime of trauma.

Our days are nearly continuous streams of
unconscious reaction:
"He looks trustworthy."
"He looks dangerous."
"I should…"
"I'm so…"
"I can't…"
"I'll just…"
"I could never…"

Why did you think that?
Did you even notice the sign you saw?
What was it?
What did you assume?

How many signs do we obey
without even noticing?

Signs only have power if
you don't reflect on them.
Notice them,
in the street and in your mind,
and reflect on them.
Take your power back.

Next time you see the "don't walk" light
and no cars are coming
you could just stand there
or you could cross
or you could fall to your knees and sob
and roll around in the street.

Whatever you do,
first, wake up.

Who Are These Artists?

Who are these artists
that work so hard to
make their ideas into objects
or print or performance or sound?
What do they want?
Why don't they do something else
with the possibilities
of their brief existence?

How many will look back on a lifetime
of wasted efforts, wasted time,
opportunities lost,
potential selves, life paths, and loves sacrificed
as they find themselves
old, poor, and alone
surrounded by their "art,"
monuments of their failure to actually live?

How many will be saved
by sacrificing their idea of being an artist
and instead of trying to make a whole life
out of art
make their art while living a whole life?

Young Love Forever

The old fisherman walks the shore,
steady, patient, and quiet,
working to make peace with life,
a bit before the sunset.

His wife has passed away
and his children are grown
and somewhere else
they have lives of their own.

Alone
he must make his peace.

He is almost soft and empty enough,
at last,
for the fullness of life
to fit and breathe
comfortably inside of him.

But the old fisherman shakes his head
and smiles, a little sad,
as his longing taunts his surrender.

He gently steps along the line
where waves and sand
have playfully wrestled
in young love forever.

The Mess

Sometimes the poem knocks and you feel hassled,
as if you have something better to do,
like sleep or work.

But a poem is a purge
and you have much to purge.

There can be no such thing
as excess of poetry from you,
for years.

So grab your pen
and dig out the mess.

Examine the mess
and the hole it came from.

Firefly

I used to have a saying,
"It's always darkest
just before
it gets even darker."

It came to me
while blindly,
awkwardly stumbling
through freezing, starless night.
Night without end.

Without premonition
I abruptly find myself
standing in a brilliant clearing
and as I shudder and sob and laugh
and all the confusion
and turmoil
and fear
fall off,

I look behind
and the way I came in utter darkness
is now a gold-lit path.

I now understand how
it all had purpose,
all of it
pulling me with perfect grace and certainty.

If I had chosen what I was doing
and where I was going
I would have never come
to the right place.

There was a path
even when I didn't think there was a ground
beneath my next
s
s
s
t
e...

p.

My guide was a firefly,
a humble, diligent, wise point of light,
from nothingness appearing
just long enough to indicate the way
to stumble
just a little further
before fading back into the immersing shadow

Now, as I struggle along through darkness
I remember that everything is revealed
in hindsight,
and hindsight has at last given me
this foresight:

though I don't know where I'm going
or how I'll get there,
I will arrive at precisely the right place
and then I will understand why it had to be so.

The nights are so long
and the days but moments,

but now I can trust the darkness
and the firefly.
I can breathe deeply,
and laugh,
while blindly,
awkwardly stumbling
through freezing, starless night.

A Blessing for You

May you be happy.
May you feel light.
May you allow a smile to gently spread
through your face.
May your eyes be open and clean.

May you release your apprehension
and be filled with supple strength.

May you stand tall and rooted,
pulled taught from above and below.

May you remember that your appearance
comes from the inside out.

May you remember that you're someone
who people are pleased to meet.

May you never forget that you are lovable.
May you often relive memories
of the love you have known.

May you remember that the purest happiness
is there inside you, always shining
just behind the clouds;
may you fly beyond them
on the gust of a single thought.

Why?

Looking for Connections

    I am lonely. I have wonderful family, friends, colleagues, and loving relationships of many kinds. Yet I am lonely, and I suffer from it. I also suffer from despair. Some say this is the human condition, but I disagree. I think it's a wide-spread, social, cultural, and political condition and I live in constant rebellion against it.

This book is for me to express my deepest self publicly. I am testing the idea that I can overcome loneliness and despair by opening my inner world and inviting others in. Maybe, in turn, you will want to invite me into yours.

I live in Seattle. If you're local, maybe we should hang out. You can contact me through my website and maybe we will want to meet.

(JSYK: I'm picky about who I spend my time with. Part of the reason I struggle with loneliness is that many people just want to feed on my attention and energy, so I have developed appropriate defenses. I don't want to be around people who leave me feeling depleted. I want relationships that energize everyone involved; otherwise I prefer solitude.)

I hope that you will reach out to me if you would like to collaborate on writing or music or visual art or theater/film or zines, anything that will help us feel alive, connected, significant, and purposeful. Let's tear down the alienating, reifying spectacle of capitalism. We can begin by ripping just one section of the fabric, the one that keeps you and me apart.

Find more of my work and contact me at:

BeBoldeBeWyse.com
Facebook: Ben Gallup
Instagram: @bengallup
Twitter: @ben_gallup

www.ingramcontent.com/pod-product-compliance
Lightning Source LLC
Chambersburg PA
CBHW060504080526
44584CB00015B/1536